Imagining Things
and other poems

Our world of animals, seasons and landscapes
is full of magic and mystery. It's an enchanted
kingdom of birds and beasts and secret places,
which can be there for all of us every day.

Kenneth Steven's new collection of lyrical
and often humorous poems shows some of the
surprise and excitement that can be ours in the
world around us. Read these poems to discover
the joy and wonder of imagining things.

Kenneth Steven lives in Perthshire and is a
poet, novelist, and tutor of creative writing. He
has over 20 books in print. He regularly appears
at literary festivals and runs school workshops
around the UK.

Best wishes,

Kenneth Steven

For Andrew McNab, and to remember my father,
Campbell Steven, who gave me a love
of all things living

Imagining
Things and other poems

Kenneth Steven

illustrated by Caroline Pedler

LION
CHILDREN'S

A Lion Children's Book
an imprint of
Lion Hudson plc
Mayfield House, 256 Banbury Road,
Oxford OX2 7DH, England
www.lionhudson.com
ISBN 0 7459 4907 X

First edition 2005
10 9 8 7 6 5 4 3 2 1 0

A catalogue record for this book is available
from the British Library

Typeset in 12/14 Latin 725 BT
Printed and bound in Great Britain
by Cox & Wyman Ltd, Reading

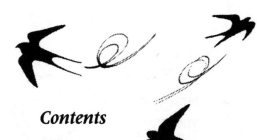

Contents

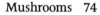

Wishing

I wish I'd been the very first person
On the very first day of the world
To see the sun rise for the very first time
On the very first morning there was.

I wish I'd watched the very first flower
Open out for the very first time.
I wish I'd heard the very first bird
Sing the very first song to say thank you.

Imagining things

Saturday morning and the skies are grey;
Danny sits in his bedroom six floors up,
His eyes downcast and his elbows on the sill,
Listening to the grey rain sing:

It's singing from the chimneys
And it's singing from the roofs
It's singing from the steeples
And it's singing from the trees.

He wanted to go and play football,
But Jamie's got a cold and Alfie's away,
Sam's at his granny's and Alan hasn't time,
And Danny's mum said: 'It's far too wet!'

It's singing from the chimneys
And it's singing from the roofs
It's singing from the steeples
And it's singing from the trees.

Danny imagines he's a bird,
Flying up over the houses and away,
Looking down on all the little figures,
Scampering away with their brollies and their hats.

It's singing from the chimneys
And it's singing from the roofs
It's singing from the steeples
And it's singing from the trees.

Now in his mind he's a thousand miles away,
Riding on a camel through yellow desert sand,
Searching for a treasure that's been lost since time
   began –
And he has to find it soon...

Danny isn't here in a city block of flats,
Danny isn't sitting with his elbows on the sill,
Danny isn't wishing he is out there in the rain –
Danny's far away – imagining things!

Seeing in the dark

At night
Creak open your window to listen.

A car
Hums away and disappears.

The church bell
Echoes softly eleven times.

Two cats
Sing angry songs to each other,

Till someone shoos them away
And a bin lid rattles.

Then there's just the wind
Lifting and hissing the trees.

A house sign creaks
In the last bit of breeze.

The last light goes out –
There's not a single sound.

Attention please

Ladies and gentlemen
A robin will be landing at terminal three
In approximately four minutes.
Would all sparrows still requiring breakfast
Please proceed to the bird table immediately
As a crow is expected to arrive
At any moment. The blue tit who left his
  luggage
Over by the back window
Is kindly asked by security to remove it.
We wish you all a very pleasant flight.

Trincomalee

Nobody knows the name Trincomalee
But we dream of it night after night;
Dark waves on a shore and silvery lamps
That shine from a hillside so bright.

Trincomalee has tigers and snakes,
Elephants shadow the trees,
And crocodiles' eyes shine white in the swamps
(They say there are sharks in the seas).

And deep in our dreams of Trincomalee
We smell oranges heavy and full
That grow in dark glades where the moonlight
   is sweet
And the lagoons all lie silent and cool.

Trincomalee smells of cinnamon gold
It smells of saffron and silk.
The night tastes of grapes, of melon and dates,
Of mango and coconut milk.

To tell you the truth, we've been there each night,
Since ever we started to be;
We've climbed in the trees, we've swum in the pools,
We've grown up in Trincomalee.

Trincomalee is a place in Sri Lanka. This poem was written before the
devastating tsunami in December 2004.

Bruno

When a bear comes blearily out of sleep
He blinks and blinks in the sunlight.

There's blue sky! All around
The streams are babbling with snow
   and stories.

He's big as a barn. One paw
Could break down a door.

He has bad breath. He's been curled in a ball
For a hundred and twenty-two nights.

He's had Bed –
But now he wants Breakfast.

Home sweet home

Rooks make nests in towers
And owls in ancient trees;
Robins build in river banks
But where do cuckoos nest?

Swifts build under house roofs
And herons up high trees;
Divers go to islands
But where do cuckoos nest?

Some birds will use a kettle
And others build in sheds;
I've heard of eggs in attic lofts,
But where do cuckoos nest?

Swallows

When winter is over
And spring has pushed up green
From the sleeping ground,
The swallows come back.

One morning they're there again;
Little black streamers with forked tails,
Trapeze artists, zigzagging from wire to wire,
Whizzing over our heads.

They fly all the way from Africa –
Thousands and thousands of miles –
And return to the very same street
They left at the end of autumn.

Each one of them
Weighs less than the smallest coin.

Dawn

He painted the gold on the underside of the
    eagle's wings,
He put the bounce into the kangaroo;
He wove the peacock's tail of many colours,
And told the geese the way to Iceland.

He let the lions purr when they were happy,
He gave the kingfisher a coat of royal blue.
He made the otter from a piece of running water,
And put a silver voice into the nightingale's throat.

He coloured the sky with orange and silver;
He asked the birds to sing before the day began –
And he gave it all free, to be loved and enjoyed,
Looked after for ever, his priceless new world.

Our Corrie

By day he is all softness –
One long ginger curve –
Lying like a piece of orange
In the middle of a rug.

Those gentle blue eyes!
Everyone who comes to the house
Falls in love at once
With our gorgeous fluffy beast.

But after dark
He leaves the cat door,
Becomes the terror of the town –
A law unto himself.

What yowlings and caterwaulings
We hear at midnight,
As our sleepy softie
Turns into a tyrant.

Tabby cats and Manx cats,
Persian blues and Siamese –
All of them are terrified
By our ginger tom.

But in the morning
As the postman brings our mail,
Our warrior comes back home
Without one single scratch.

He flops down on the carpet
In a warm patch of light,
And waits for his admirers
To welcome him back home.

Secret things

I know an island
Where the wind blows all year;
The rain is hard as stone
As it blows across the hills.

Day and night it's stormy,
The sea all around is rough,
And walking anywhere at all
Means going against the wind.

But here's what's so amazing –
Each springtime little buds
Of flowers coloured green and blue
And scarlet lift their heads.

They peep between the stones
And open out their leaves;
They nod their tiny heads
As if they're waving in the wind.

And the whole island changes –
Instead of being grey,
It turns into a patchwork quilt
Of all the finest hues.

In the beginning

I've watched a spider at first light
Building his web of gold;
I've seen an otter swim and play –
But why did God make toads?

I like to hear the tawny owl
Or watch a swallow's shows;
I look for cuckoos, jays and wrens
But must we have the crows?

Still, I suppose if all of us
Got rid of our pet hates,
There'd soon be not a creature left,
(Nor us and all our mates).

For some it's mice, while some loathe snakes,
And some hate wriggling worms;
And some hate rats and others frogs,
And some each thing that squirms.

So maybe we should see that God
Made each thing great and small,
And loves each one just as it is –
As much as he loves us all.

Oystercatchers

Whenever the new year comes around
I always count the days
To the return of the oysties.

All winter they stay at the coast
But on a certain day in spring
They fly back up the river.

I wake up at four in the morning
To hear a great piping
As the first birds appear.

They always come in flocks
Like gangs of bright children
With loud shrieks of laughter.

Long orange bills and quick wings,
Dark heads and beady eyes –
The clowns of the river.

I always know that spring's arrived
When I hear that first one piping
All along the river.

Dreams

A caterpillar was asked
What he wanted to be when he grew up.
'A butterfly,' he answered.
How they laughed and laughed.

'You're not going to be some special thing
With beautiful wings!
You're going to help with the gardening,'
His father told him sternly.

The caterpillar took off his shoes (all fifty pairs)
And tried not to cry,
As he counted cabbages
To get some sleep.

But that autumn
He knitted himself a jumper
And closed his eyes –
He had to believe it was true.

And one spring morning
He woke up feeling new.
He flew through the window –
A butterfly at last.

Tadpoles

One day I found some jelly with dots in it
In a drain by the side of the road.

I scraped it up and took it home,
Kept it in a glass of water.

But then the dots started wriggling,
Became little tiny commas,

Strange creatures with tails –
I thought I'd discovered Martians!

I fed the commas with cat food
And they gobbled it up like lightning;

I let them out into the sink at night
After Mum and Dad were asleep.

Then all of a sudden they grew legs,
Started bouncing all over the place.

I had no choice now but to confess
I had frogs in the bathroom sink!

Mum sighed. (She'd been wondering
Where so much of the cat food had gone.)

'At least they aren't meowing,'
She said, as we drove to the duck pond.

We carried out armfuls of frogs
And I waved goodbye on the grass.

Sometimes I go back even now
With a tin of cat food at night

And I can hear them jumping for joy
As they smell their very first food!

The field mouse

On a lawn in front of the river
In the buttery yellow warmth of April –
A field mouse, busy eating.

I went down to his level;
He sat up on two paws and looked, wondering,
All quivering in the wind.

He would only have filled an eggcup;
No more than a scrap of fur
Followed by a length of tail.

I stretched out a finger and touched him
Soft as a leaf, yet he staggered, toppled,
Then trundled off afraid into the trees.

I learned that morning
Something I will not forget –
That gentleness is not as easy as we think.

What am I?

I go softly on my stomach so no one will see when I STING!

The puzzle

Where does the wind come from?
We feel it in our hair,
We watch it on the sea
And yet we cannot touch it.

Where does the wind come from?
It knocks against our windows,
It shakes the strongest branches
And yet we cannot catch it.

Where does the wind come from?
Sometimes it isn't there.
The sky just holds its breath
And yet we cannot hold it.

Where does the wind come from?
It bangs about our houses
And rages through our gardens
And yet we cannot calm it.

Where does the wind begin?
Where does the wind end?
No one knows the answer
But the wind is always there.

Flying a kite

On bright and blustery days in spring
Dad tells me to get my kite.
I go up to the attic and bring it down
(A golden eagle, as big as me).

Outside the wind is like a giant puppy;
Running up behind, then leaping out
   of nowhere,
Knocking me over in one great bounce –
But Dad keeps hold of my hand.

By the time we battle to the top of the hill
I am all out of breath and the trees are bent;
The sky is scudding with big, fluffy clouds –
It feels like the roof of the world.

We let the eagle go –
Suddenly it grows as strong as a horse
And both of us are nearly blown away
As the eagle flutters thirty metres high.

We go back home when the sun is sinking
And we can't lift our arms any longer.
We fall asleep on the couch together
With our eagle on the floor beside us.

The kittens

I went into a barn
At the very start of spring;
The snow was falling outside
Like big, wet lashes.

It was warm and dark inside
And the air smelled of straw.
All at once I heard mewing
From over in the far corner.

Three newborn kittens
Searched about in the darkness,
Their eyes still blind, like cuts,
In the soft fur of their heads.

I picked one up very gently
And it was just a bag of milk;
I held it close to my jumper,
Softly stroked its tummy.

At once its whole body
Was filled with the sound of purring,
A roaring as it buried its claws
In the deep wool of my jumper.

Those three kittens were named
Bumble, Panda and Dan;
They're still on the hill farm
And they still know how to purr.

Now and again

When I wake early in the morning
And I can't get back to sleep
I listen to the songbirds
As dawn begins to peep.

A blackbird sings from the rooftop
With a voice so rich and clear,
Thanking God for the morning,
For all that is precious here.

The river's tale

The river in spring
Starts young and strong
All blue and shiny.

But the river in summer
Goes quiet and dry
Is tired and lazy.

The river in autumn
Is as wild as a horse
Riding the rocks in a galloping frenzy.

The river in winter
Is all crisp and glassy
With ice in its eddies.

The river at night
Whispers and smiles
On its run to the sea.

Mr O'Malley

Every evening I sit at the window
And watch the flats all around.
The lights of the city twinkle and glint
As the sky grows purply black.

On the other side of the street
Lives old Mr O'Malley;
His legs are bad so he can't go out –
He sleeps for most of the day.

But at night he opens his window wide.
He sits at the sill and waits
As birds fly in from all around,
Bringing him things in their beaks.

Magpies come with wonderful things –
Gold and precious stones
They've picked from dressers, from jewellery boxes –
They've carried them back for him.

Mr O'Malley smiles as they come,
He strokes their velvety heads,
And as I look up his room shines bright
With all the treasure that's his.

So even though he never goes out,
Even though he just lives in one room,
Mr O'Malley has seen the world
Through the things that the magpies bring.

The moon

The moon can be a fingernail
Up in a blue-grey sky.

The moon can be made of cobwebs
There on a June afternoon.

The moon can be full of honey
When the harvest fields are ripe.

The moon can be like a football
Kicked up from behind the hills.

The moon can be like the eye
Of an old man watching the world.

Legend

The dragon lies at the heart of the mountain,
One gold eye like a coin
Watching.

He has been there since the day
Stars began winking. He is as old
As the dust of volcanoes.

The dragon is bigger than all his enemies
Put together. He has eaten cities,
He has chewed on humans.

The dragon has not slept
For two hundred and sixty-four years –
He is hungry...

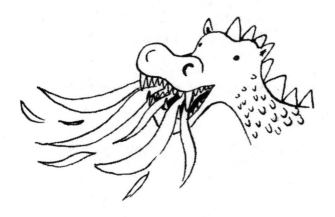

Whale

Down
In the dark
Belly of the sea
Whale sings.

Like a longship
She steers
Through the blue
Night and day.

Her songs
Are eerie, lonely,
Of caves and shells,
Of secrets and dreams,

Of legends
And great, white
Atlantis.
The oldest songs in the world.

Undersong

here

    under

              the

          sea

     dark

      deep

      down

the

whale

    booms

      lonely

and nobody hears

A poem for whispering

The night is approaching
Long shadows now creep;
Through meadow and woodland
The dark stretches deep.

Up in the sky
The stars burn all pearl-white
And out from the hill edge
The moon climbs quite milk-bright.

Villages shine
Like clusters of fish
In a vast, shadowed ocean
With only one wish:

To float to the morning
So far out of view
Safe, sound and sleeping
Till the sun is made new.

Remember

Life is about the little things,
The gemstones round our feet.

Being woken by sunlight,
The cherry scent of the springtime.

Going into the morning forest for kindling,
The sun slanting like beams from the sky.

Feeding a robin in February snow,
Listening to the bright jewellery of his song.

Watching someone coming home from school
With a handful of chestnuts and a long story.

Listening to the great spirit of the wind
Wrestling with the trees all through the night.

Laughing at the huge thrashing of rain,
Running and laughing through the autumn rain.

The dream mare

Every night when I was a boy
A horse came into my room;
Its breath was sweet with hay and grass,
It shone in the light of the moon.

And so I climbed onto its back
And we flew through the window wide;
I felt the dust of the stars on my face
As we rose on our cosmic ride.

I looked down on rivers that fell to the sea
On mountains that rose so high;
I glimpsed the shimmer of ice-bright peaks
As darkness went gusting by.

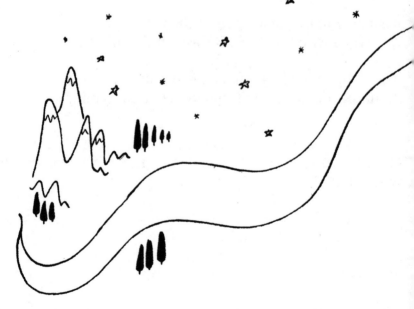

I saw wolves and bears and great herds of deer
I watched wild swans rise into the air;
I glimpsed the backs of whales in the sea
As I gripped the mane of the mare.

Then in the end a red spark appeared
On the very far edge of the night;
My horse turned back and headed for home
With wing-beats steady and bright.

I woke up at dawn in my own room once more
With wonderful words in my head;
A scent of hay left still in the room
And hoof-prints beside the bed.

Wild goose chase

Under a bridge
Something like a print.

A paw, perhaps, passed by
At midnight, padding

North, and leaving
Just a hint of fish.

Trail all day,
Catch glimpses, ripples

That could be,
Might be

The tail of an otter
Playing Houdini,

Melted into water
Gone to ground – vanished.

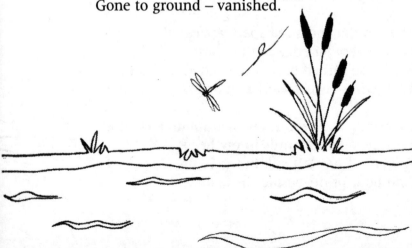

Otter

The otter
Is water
Come to life.

He plays
With the river
Like a toy,

Is stronger
Than a whole ocean
Full of tides,

Scents a fish
Far away
Downstream

And finds it
Swift and sure
With his nose.

The well

light   green   dappled   water   well

well   water   light   dappled   green

dappled   well   green   light   water

green   dappled   water   well   light

water   light   well   green   dappled

The mouse's tale

I am a mouse:
Terrified of everything –
I only come out at night.

I eat in a terrible hurry
Then dash underground –
Just in case someone sees me.

My mother and father
Were caught by an owl
Who gulped them in one go.

I have sleepless nights
Worrying about cats and traps,
Wishing I was big and strong.

How lucky everyone else is –
Nobody knows
How awful it is being a mouse!

The Maker

In the beginning
Who made this world?

Who gave the nightingale its song,
And put the orange on a robin's throat?

Who gave the horse its whinny
And lit the furthest star?

Who made a wren weigh less
Than one single tiny coin,

But with a voice that was as sweet
As the finest singer ever?

Who made the geese
Fly all the way home in winter?

Who made the salmon leap the rivers each October?
Last of all, who made us –

And asked us to look after his creation,
To be his hands on earth.

And who is still asking us the same thing
All this time later?

Bats

On summer nights
I pad outside in my slippers
To watch for bats.

The river's smooth as silk –
Whispering as it searches
Slow towards the sea.

The midges dance their jigs
In still, blue air –
Weave over the glassy water.

A bat! Over there – and there,
Like soft bits of felt,
Ghosting across the pools.

Sometimes they flit round my ears
Or over my feet –
But they never touch me.

By morning they've gone,
Slipped away to attics and caves
To sleep upside down.

Calculations

When I was still at school
One summer afternoon
A ladybird crossed my jotter
While I was doing sums.

I almost brushed it away
Crossly with the back of my hand,
When suddenly I thought to myself,
'Maybe it's off on holiday.

'Maybe it's gone to relatives
It hasn't seen for years;
Maybe they're off to the blackboard
To draw things with their feet.

'Maybe they'll play with the duster
And roll about with the chalk.
This is their summer holiday,
They need one as much as me.'

Taking the plunge

Swimming in the Atlantic
Is the bravest thing you can do.

On a blue day in July
You go and hide in a sand dune,

Change into your costume
As the goose bumps begin to swell.

You go down onto the beach
And pretend you don't feel the wind,

Put a first toe in the water
And it feels as if buckets of snow

Have been poured into your leg.
You smile at all those behind you

And give them a little wave,
Even though inside you're wincing

And wishing they'd all go away.
You take a first step to be brave

And the cold of Greenland and Iceland
Goes shooting up to your head.

Your legs feel like they're wood
And your teeth clatter and shake;

You've no more blood in your feet
And your hands are like pieces of ice,

As a blue wave comes rushing to meet you
And knocks you right off your feet.

You swallow half the Atlantic,
Get sand in your nose and mouth,

Swim for a few frantic moments,
Then get washed in like a bit of wood.

Your friends come running to find you,
Asking you what it was like

And shaking all over you stand,
Grinning at the edge of the tide:

'It's lovely once you get in.
Really and truly I mean it!'

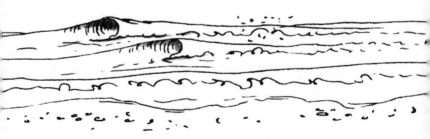

Stick-in-the-mud

The slug was the last
  To slink into the Ark.

  (Maybe you think
    He should have been left behind.)

    But Noah waited
      Patiently as ever

      Till the slug had slipped in
        And the great door closed.

      But the slug had got wet
        From the first drops of rain;

        The slug was soaked through
          From sliding in the mud,

And ever since
The slug

h
  a
   s
   l
   e
   f
   t
   a
   t
   r
   a
   i
 l
  b
   e
     h
     i
     n
    d
     h
      i
      m

Everywhere he goes.

A rhyme for the sun

All day
Sarah wanted to play.

But the rain came down
And buried the town.

It smudged out the steeple
And soaked all the people,

It sang and it glittered
Till Sarah felt bitter.

But then as she stood
In a very bad mood

Watching the rain
Course down the pane

A small edge of gold
Peeped from the fold

Of a great heavy cloud.
She gasped out loud

As a rainbow arched full
Over the school,

Over the houses and over the shops
And the rain had stopped.

Sarah went dashing
Her Wellingtons splashing

To play with her friends.
She came round a bend

And there was the sun –
The day had begun.

Tide-dancing

Collecting things from the sea
Is about being patient...

There's a shell!
Closer, closer, and just a bit further –

Whumph! Your left leg's soaked
And you've water up one sleeve.

You limp back beaten,
But the sun has sympathy,

Slowly dries you up. You creep back...
There's something yellow there,

All strange and shiny.
Maybe it's a coin

Washed in from a treasure ship
Years and years ago!

Careful now. The sea's breathing
Soft and gentle. One step more and...

Got it! Just some rotten silver paper
From a mouldy old biscuit!

You run back safe
And a wave roars in behind you.

Then you see it. A starfish
As small as your little nail.

It's beautiful. You have to have it.
Your heart goes like a drum.

If you jump from that rock
To that one, then maybe...

But what if you took off your shoes?
No, there's too much glass.

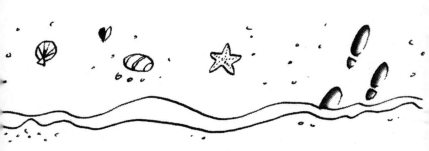

All right, first jump –
The sea's black and waiting.

Second jump – you teeter,
Both feet on the same tiny rock.

You reach out into space
And *crash*!

You're soaked from head to foot
With another wave coming.

But at least you're going home
With the best starfish ever!

The sea

'What's the sea like?' Susie asked.
Her grandfather was hammering a shelf
Onto the living room wall –
He'd been a fisherman all his life.

'The sea's rough and the sea's cold,
The sea's grey and it's never calm.'
Susie's grandfather looked at her sternly,
And it wasn't at all what she'd hoped.

'What's the sea like?' Susie asked
Her auntie one evening at tea.
Aunt Fiona had run a little shop
On the sea front all her life.

'The sea's dirty and the sea's busy,
The sea's boring and it's always noisy.'
Susie's auntie looked at her sternly,
And it wasn't at all what she'd hoped.

'What's the sea like?' Susie asked
Her friend Sonya who came from Jamaica.
Sonya smiled and her whole face
Was filled with beautiful light.

'The sea is blue and the sea is shining,
The sea is alive and always changing.'
Susie looked at her friend and nodded
For that was all she had hoped.

Thunderstorm

It was August
And the days were hot and sticky
Like strawberry jam.

The cottage we stayed in was stuffy.
I tossed and turned all night,
Watched the stars crackling in my skylight window.

One day the air was orange;
There wasn't a breath of wind,
The only sound the soft flicker of the river.

All day we seemed to wait,
Even though we didn't know why or for what –
I sat with my feet in the river.

Then, at six o'clock,
A tiny glow-worm
Wriggled above the hilltops.

I ran inside and watched from the window
As lightning crackled and shone in silver
Till my big eyes blinked with it.

Then the rain came at last,
Singing and shining in great, fat drops
Till everything was shining bright.

The following day the skies opened wide –
Blue and beautiful –
The river full of new stories.

Listen

The deer has ears that hear the smallest sound.
The deer can hear a single twig crack –
She is gone in a single bound.
As soft and still as a breath.

Sounds to me

When pigeons fly upwards from trees
Their wings whisper softly into nowhere.

When swans lift off from a river or a lake
They sound like great wind instruments flying.

When geese struggle back at last for winter
They sound like distant bagpipes being tuned.

When sparrows gather for their morning crumbs
They sound like a bunch of Italian tourists.

When crows perch high on chimney pots and roofs
They sound like old, bad-tempered grandpas.

When I open my ears and open my eyes
Everything seems so exciting to me.

By degrees

Ladies' tummies murmur
Gentlemen's stomachs grumble
But lions' bellies BELLOW!

Wasps

That August the wasps invaded
Like a gang of bikers.
In their yellow and black jackets
They drizzled the air, zoomed around corners.

In the endless hot blue afternoons,
They crawled into jam and across plates,
Bashed windows and went at full throttle
Around cafés and swarms of tourists.

Until one day the skies turned orange
And the air hung in misty curtains,
Heavy and hot as wool. Very far away
Thunder prowled about the hills like bears.

A gull sailed away making a sound
Like an old bicycle wheel; a flicker of lightning
Squirmed above the woods, and suddenly,
Rain began falling in great drops.

Next morning, the wasps were dead;
Outside hotels and shops their crisp hulls lay
Like curled leaves. They blew away
Through the lanes, were washed into wet
    September ditches.

Wanting away

When I was at school
All I looked at were the trees.
I saw them shingle with sunlight
As the sums went up on the board.

Everything smelled of chalk;
I wanted to run in the woods,
Explore until it was dark –
Come back with stories.

The clock ticked so slowly,
Minute by minute went past,
As the light changed from orange to silver,
And the wind rushed through the woods.

'Are you doing your sums?'
Miss MacCallum shouted at me.
I went red and stared at my jotter,
The numbers whirled round in my head.

I wished the bell would go
So I could pack my satchel and race
Out into the autumn sunlight,
Go wherever I wanted to go.

One day I knew I'd be free,
I'd never do sums again;
I'd run and run in the woods,
And come home with my very own stories.

Sheepdog

The sheepdog is a black-and-white waterfall,
Able to flatten like a wave in the field,
His eyes blue pools.

The sheep huddle together in boulders
As he runs rings around them,
Ties them into a knot.

He knows every whistle the shepherd gives;
His brains are in his paws –
He is as wise as his grandfather.

At night he lies like a rug before the fire,
His eyes far away in another world –
Dreaming of cats.

The rat

I like going out with my friends
Late at night.
I like going to places that smell –
Drains and dustbins.

We make as much noise as we like
When we're out in the dark.
Nobody can catch us
We hide every time.

Maybe you think we're not there –
But you're wrong.
A rat's never further away
Than behind your bedroom wall.

Mushrooms

When sunlight was blowing about
Like a wild puppy

And autumn had painted the trees
In vivid golds and reds

We went for a drive
On a road that wound into nowhere.

All at once we spotted a field of mushrooms –
Like little gnomes with white hats.

We got out and picked them,
Carried them back to the car.

They broke like new bread –
Their hats and their stalks.

Underneath they had pink frills
As smooth as silk.

We took them home
And made the best omelette ever.

We fried those mushrooms
Till they squeaked and squealed in the pan.

They melted in our mouths –
Soft and sweet and buttery.

Geese

One evening there was a noise
Like the rusty wheel of a bicycle.

The boys stopped playing football
And looked up into the autumn sky.

Mrs O'Grady who was washing her dishes
Up on the eighteenth floor peered out.

The commuters who were waiting in the traffic
Looked up and listened and watched.

They had all been so busy,
Running and buying and shouting and counting

They had forgotten that this was the day
The geese came back from Iceland.

It was like a fairytale in their heads,
The story of the geese coming home –

And the city lay awake all night,
Remembering.

To hear a tiger purring

When I was eight
I dreamed each night
Of far away
In India.

In emerald fields
With silken winds
All around the trees
Whispered and hissed.

I saw white walls
And temple rocks;
Bright peacocks shrieked
From sacred glades;

Lily leaves
In shifting pools –
A golden nose,
A golden eye.

Then at last
I stretched my head,
I held my breath –
To hear a tiger purring.

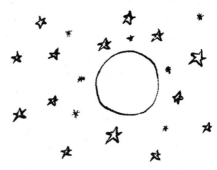

The world from the window

One night when I was five
Dad carried me up on his shoulders
To the loft at the top of the house.

It smelled of apples and old boxes
And I heard the wind outside
Shaking the autumn trees.

Dad stretched and opened the skylight window,
Poked me up through the gap
Into the inky night.

Right over the edge of the sky
The moon was rising like some great white ball
Or the eye of a giant.

And I watched it
Climbing into the darkness
Through mountains of cloud

As the stars tingled above me
In millions and millions
On that magic night in autumn.

The adventure

Last year
I went fishing for the first time.

It was October
And the rivers were roaring with rain;

Everything was leaves and mud,
It got dark at four o'clock.

I was so excited
I felt I could hardly breathe.

We walked to the top of the hill
And there in between the trees

I saw the flash of the waterfall
Coming down like a horse's tail.

We got our lines ready
And threw them over the bridge,

We held the handles
Tight till our knuckles gleamed.

An owl floated over our heads
Like a huge, soft moth.

The rain began to fall
Like big, hard stones.

'I've got one!' I shouted. 'I'm sure!'
I felt the tug on the line,

And frantic I reeled it in,
Till the silver trout was jumping

Like a magic thing in the dark.
My very first fish.

Conkers

Somehow we always knew
When the conkers were finally ready.
There was just something different,
A certain scent in the air.

That night the wind grew like a giant,
Rocked the house and toppled the leaves
From all the trees in the street.
I lay awake, listening and thinking.

The moon rode through the clouds
Like some great silver galleon.
I dreamed of pirates and gold,
Of my very own treasure island.

I woke with a start and knew
It was six o'clock in the morning.
I pulled on my clothes and crept
Out into the empty street.

The wind played hide and seek.
For a long time it was quiet,
Then all of a sudden it boomed
From behind someone's garden gate.

I was blown all the way up the hill
In the early morning light.
There was the chestnut tree
And I was the first one there.

They lay all round my feet
Like bright, new-polished buttons.
Mahogany things half-hidden
By twigs and new-fallen leaves.

I crammed every pocket
With as many as I could carry.
My very own treasure –
I felt richer than any king.

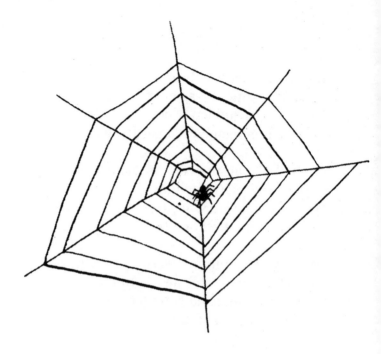

Web

High up in the wind of the wood
The spider spins and sews
A magic carpet of strings
That leads from branch to branch.

In the morning
Each strand dances with dew
And in every gleaming pearl
A new sun shines.

Sometimes

In
all
the
rush
and
hurry
of
our
lives
we
need
so
much
just
now
and
then
to
find
an

        island

Changing our ways

The city has come to a standstill;
Everywhere cars are honking
Like strange birds lost in clouds.

The city is under a blanket of fog;
People feel their way home
Street by street, as if they were blind.

Fog is like candyfloss –
It's orange and grey and tastes
All thick and gritty.

I stand at the window and watch;
It makes me think how helpless we are
In something as simple as fog.

Everybody slows down,
Starts talking to each other –
Maybe it should be foggy every day.

The city fox

He is the colour of ginger,
Blackberry eyes and a long wet nose
That can smell a chicken supper
Three streets away.

He moves quieter than a shadow,
Is gone in one jump so there's nothing
   left behind
Except a tell-tale smell
And a bit of tummy fluff.

His cubs are orange balls of down,
Tangles of scrapping and yapping
That grow up trusting nothing,
With enemies all around.

Wherever you are in the city
A fox is watching you.

Bonfire night

November smelled of old leaves and fog,
Of conkers and crab apples;
The river was fierce and white,
Like some runaway horse.

Nic and I went everywhere
Gathering branches and leaves
To build the biggest of all bonfires
At the bottom of the garden.

The days passed as slowly as the school clock.
In the kitchen, Mum bubbled things on the stove
And Dad kept strange packages in the hall.
We had waited so long it hurt.

Then bonfire night came at last.
We padded out into the shadows,
The stars crackling above us
Like hundreds of tiny bonfires.

A match was scratched alight;
In a moment the dragon was roaring,
Whizzing and banging as sparks flew out
And smoke billowed the sky.

We wrote our names with sparklers,
Drank spicy drinks that burned our throats.
Dad fizzed fireworks into the air
That burst into all kinds of flowers.

We wandered to bed at long past midnight,
Dizzy, the glow of the fire in our eyes.
We woke next morning, half-remembering,
The taste of ash in our mouths.

Alumbria

In the morning
It is spinklebright.

The wind thrums at the trees
With their red, gold and amber leaves.

The river goes downstream like a humberback,
White horses over rocks and banks.

A skiffle of moon hangs in the sky,
The sky that is blue as ice.

Children run and jamble in the field,
Their faces red and full of laughter.

It is Alumbria. The time between the falling
Of the first conker and the first snowflake.

Frosty mornings

Diamonds on the windowsill,
Puddles made of white ice
That crackle underfoot.

Cars are glistening.
Drivers are scraping the glass
To make black shiny holes.

The roads are all slidy.
The postman falls on his bottom,
Scatters seventy-eight letters.

Our breath clouds the air,
Comes out in long trails
Like dragon smoke.

Inside the classroom
We write our names
On the steamed-up windows.

The slide

We longed for the sharp crinkle of December stars,
That ghostly mist like cobwebs in the grass –
Ten degrees below zero.

After the snow came petalling from the skies,
Settled into a deep quilt, the frost
Diamonded the top, making a thick crust.

Down the long descent of the lawn
We made our slide, planed the ground
Hour after hour till it smiled with ice.

At night we teetered out with buckets,
Rushed the water down the slide's length
In one black stain.

Next day the slide was lethal,
A curling glacier that shot us downhill
In one single hiss.

Even after the thaw had greened our world again
The slide remained written in the grass
As long as our stories.

Night drive

Mum and Dad make a bed for me in the back.
The car is cosy and I creep under the rugs
Not quite wanting to go to sleep,
Listening to their voices softly talking.

And I want to get there and yet I don't;
When I rub my hand against the steamed-up
    window
I see stars and the lights of distant farms,
And I think of the children lying there asleep.

We drive up and up on a windy road,
I can see snowflakes blink against the window.
An owl comes out of the dark like a ghost,
And I catch a glimpse of its round white face.

We reach home in the end and I am carried inside
(It is all so strange in the middle of the night)
I drink hot cocoa and snuggle into bed,
And I dream of the night drive until morning.

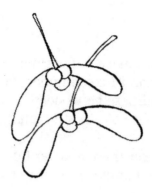

Mistletoe

Mistletoe grows in the strangest places
Far away in the woods.
Its leaves are smooth and soft as laces,
Its berries like melted ice.

No one knows how mistletoe came here,
No one knows what it means.
But everyone knows that the end of the year
Is when it grows most special.

Then it's hung from every doorway
As Christmas day comes close.
And everyone knows it's there to say
You must stand underneath and kiss.

Gathering holly

One day at the beginning of winter
Mum and I go to find holly
Down at the end of the wood.

We stand in mittens and hoods
As the snowflakes come swirling
Like giant cats' paws.

My toes are all tingling
But deep in the trees
It's warm and quite still.

The berries are as bright
As the eyes of robins –
Orange and red.

The holly's all shining
Crackly and green –
We carry home armfuls.

Holly by the fireside
Holly in the hall –
Holly for Christmas.

Robins

The Christmas card robin –
Beautiful orange tummy
And black beady eyes.

But robins are little thugs;
In the woods they put on dark glasses,
Big leather jackets – and fight.

They are the hooligans of the hedgerows,
The graffiti artists of the garden,
The bullies by the back door.

Until Christmas comes around again,
When they puff out their tummies
And look lovely for the camera.

Christmas

Christmas is prickly, shiny holly
With red berries like a robin's breast.

Christmas is big white cotton snow
Falling and falling across the world.

Christmas is red presents and warm fires,
Coming home tired with a sledge and stories.

Christmas is a place you always want to get to
And never want to leave once you're there.

Christmas is imagining turning a corner
And finding Bethlehem, the stable, the baby.

Snow

This morning winter came along
Gave everything a bright new coat.

I stood at the window and watched
As a robin left footprints on my sill.

A dog stopped by the lamp-post,
Left a bright orange pool and then ran off.

The postman came whistling up the road,
Spoiled the snow with his big, black boots.

A bus went roaring past at eight,
Leaving a trail of soot and slush.

Then the neighbours started off to work
And everything turned to dirty marzipan.

I wanted to go out and put it all right,
Begin again with everything white.

And I thought of when our world was new,
Beautiful and bright – before we spoiled it.